To Poets Torbay
for ten years of encouragement.

Acknowledgements

Agenda, Poetry Salzburg, Poetry Scotland, Poetry Cornwall, THE SHOp, Sarasvati, The Dawntreader, Anthology for Patricia Oxley (Rockingham Press), Heart Shoots (Macmillan Cancer Support anthology).

With thanks to Chrystal Tuckfield, Alec Taylor and Fred Beake, not to mention my friends at Callander and Accent on Poetry. A special thanks to Judith Taylor, who persuaded me it was time that I had a book; and to Dawn and Ronnie for publishing it.

CONTENTS

Faint Remains of Existence

SNOWDROP

There it is again
standing.
A February day so cold
it is difficult to breathe.
There have been warnings
of hypothermia and spasms,
staying put is advised.

See it blooms again,
upright.
An early afternoon so chill
it's impossible to talk.
There have been sightings
of wan sunlight and clear icicles
beside the frozen pond.

Again it is here,
endures.
A skeleton thin and noble,
it's almost unbelievable:
there, roused from hiding
thrusts its hoary head through leaf and twigs,
scantily encouraged.

VIOLET

Where is your little anxious face?
Half hid in undergrowth.

You shrink into mauve shadow
beneath shade of trembling leaves.

In the dewy dank places
where your cheeks stay always wet.

Holding up small heart shaped leaves
on frail pale stems.

Respiring sweet alluring scent,
you're found! Shy violet.

WINTER TO SPRING

I

Jasmine flowers
pale yellow suns,
fragrant in tea,
sugared on weddings cakes.
A joyful sign.

II

Spring brings hope,
sunbeams shaft the dingles.
The fern of life again curls forth,
and earth's incense assails the senses.
"Hail returning asphodel."

MAYTIME MUSICAL

Bluebells, slender girls,
poised straight and graceful,
a chorus line of thousands,
flooding the woodlands.

An extravaganza,
a water ballet sapphire,
with sequin fringed costumes,
and Leichner blue eyes.

All skimpily identical,
directed by Cecil B. DeMille,
with exact perfection sway
to The Song of May.

MADEMOISELLE DIGITALIS

Foxglove
with your freckled décolletage,
raising your campanile
into the sacred blue.

Notre Dame,
the prayers of many whispering
in your core
to ease with remedies.

Abundant in the slated valleys,
arching with your
weight of bells
above impossible slopes.

Sighting your
magnificent nodding spires,
your blushed robed beauty
dulls our pulse.

RECOLLECTING LILACS

Loving the lilacs,
spikes of purple, lilac and white,
she gathered them up in an armful
(at dusk as the shadow of the
long fingered fir tree fell across the lawn);
and took them to her bedroom,
breathing their scent all night in slumber.
Only to be told next morning
such things are unlucky.

So she never brought the lilacs of purple or white
over the doorstep again.
But if she passes lilacs in twilight
pauses;
inhales, drinks them in.

ROSE GARDEN, COCKINGTON MANOR

She stoops to scoop the
fallen petals, soft as the fingers
they curve around.

The sun drenches her silky blonde hair,
a blush of gold and pink that sways
alongside the head of Peace.
Petal gathering, busy in the timeless sun-dialled garden.

Gravelled parterres and
Italianate swags of old loose roses,
hand baked brick walls which hold
the warmth, embrace the garden,
store memories and calm the wind
to whispers.

OUT STOKE CHANGING THE FLOWERS

The pink granite grave with black mica specks
is rather showy, the only one there!
Did grandma, a milliner, choose it
for her blind mother Emily?
Nanny had a thing about bleaching grates.

The stone washed up well, and shone;
Mum arranged gold and white roses.
I sheared the grass, and cleared the sides.
We stood back and admired;
clumps of daffodils nodded approval.

Mum said that it's to remember
all family, the scattered ashes
and graves, just too far away to get to....
or those that remain uncertain.

It was satisfying looking back at the
stiff roses, not morbid at all.
Was Nanny "flinging wide the gates"
in her strong contralto at six every morning
In Paradisium, with a bunch of gold roses
and a small tepid cup of tea?

BROWN BENT

A common grass on relatively nutritious
turf, a lone stalk sprouting
from the lumpy cushions of
sheep cropped heathers.
The massive dark tor
staunch above, just distant enough
for you to be beyond
its extending fallen shadow.

There on a rare humid
winter's afternoon,
you are pushed in the breeze
and return again.
Each dainty frond captures
a sparkling moist bauble,
a crystal twinkling in the sunlight.
Mundane made magnificent.

Like shaken tears poised,
an unexpected proof,
of love or hope that only
longs to make all right again.
The broken ray lends a violet
diadem, encapsulates each drop.
A continual phenomenon
which usually goes unseen.

Today you shine! It marks
you out on the whole moor side,
but perhaps you would prefer to be
Brown Bent amongst the others.

LATE FEBRUARY, HAYTOR

…and the manic lead-weight clouds
heavily laid over and behind the brimmed
horizon of moorland hills.

They seemed to move lugubriously, yet theirs
was an ever shifting pattern of dark
splotches under-lit by silver mercury.

Contra-wise a sudden opening of
enamelled bright blue, typified by thirteenth
century paintings, framed by scrolling clouds.

It seems an overture to visions.
Rose clad Mary, Cherubim of ceaseless eye,
or a finger waving benedictions.

Yet no mighty voice comes forth!
Sunlight is the sole emergence, yet high
pitched weaving wind continues …

about, between, amongst the crevasses
of gigantic stone toes thrust upward, through
Haytor's furzy mound.

Does the moor cover a massive skeleton?
Unless the toes just appeared like the casque just
appeared, in the courtyard of Otranto's Castle.

The walkers don't notice this in the least but clamber
unconcernedly all over. Could these toes prophesy
ancestral doom only to those they are seen by?

Behind the tor, granite rails are faint remains of existence
fractured and weathered, purple heather takes root.
Honey bees will manufacture ambrosia.

The Castle of Otranto is a gothic story by Horace Walpole.

MAKING A MIDDLE ENGLISH MOBILE TEXT

Ventnor reservoir verily vast with water!
Tracks overtaken terribly with torrents teeming.
Wellingtons waded the water wondrously.
Those shabbily shod, shunned sunken trails.

TOTTIFORD RESERVOIR

Tottiford: "In Mesolithic times
a skilfully handmade flint cutter and scraper
was key to survival," said the Time Team.
I suspect stressy mother, daughter quarrels,
and moans of aches and pains were much the same.

ASH WEDNESDAY

I fret over things. Out on the moor
a mixture of wild, tamed, and semi rural.
Bales of straw, stone walls, and farm dwellings,
but higher boulders erupt the fields,
Bone Tor: heaped against blue.
The burning moor,
choking brown smoke, and heat, sometimes it jumps.
Shaggy ponies munch cinder gorse.
I think of *Whistle Down the Wind*.

FERNWORTHY RESERVOIR

Bitterly cold, bright water mirrors the sky,
wavelets lap to the ancient stone circles,
remains of once smoke filled dwellings
where people huddled, boiled herbs.

But now the air is clear and a boardwalk
raises mans' foot from the mud, at least temporarily.
Beneath the sheer dam, water cascades,
sluicing against the precision cut blocks.

Up the other side where fewer people
investigate, the trail stodgily twists, rises
through a maze of glossy rhododendrons,
until once again level with shining water.

The wind blows off the higher moor and two
cream sheep wander down from the hills.
A little later a silver-haired couple with gaiters
nod "Good morning" at a fast pace.

Meadowland edged with neglected woods,
A gate-post leans making sense of a gap; ruins of
a Victorian farm, shrouded by a century of lacy-leaves,
where dappled horses shelter, haunt the gloom.

But the indelible memory flooding that day,
was the rim of bright crimson, an amazing flourish
of hawthorn berries surrounding the reservoir.
Redder than a robins puffed out chest.

HOLNE MOOR

I hear the first cuckoo, "Cuckoo"
and it is May.
By the reservoir's verge are violets blue
hidden away.
High over the moor white clouds gather,
foals frolic in play.
Bright golden is furze, but brown the heather
on this fresh day.

Great crested grebes make courtship
and skim the lake.
Full fleeced ewes rest and their lambs skip
with playful shake.
And winter has lost its ice held grip;
sunbathes the snake.

With ink-black sheen down flaps the rook,
he blinks and struts,
tugs unseen things and round him looks
between the tufts.
Then spirals up, to rocky tor and croaks
"I know enough."

MIDSUMMER'S DREAM, POSTBRIDGE

"Would buttercups be real gold
and their centrings of yellow diamonds,
this simple thing formed of frivolity
a diadem fit for a kingly head could be bestowed?"

The Oak heard poems he thought not so old,
the wind took its path through the rustling leaves,
and cast shaky shadows to the moist river grasses,
fluting the reeds below where they rested.

Titania, her gossamer wings invisibly folded,
skirt floating wide upon the damp sward,
green as to green in equality blended, brought
strawberries wild to quench in their juiciness.

The sun slanting low under doubled stone bridges,
evening dusk came all bird song and thistledown,
poetry fades, for the play is but temporal, yet the
stream noisily cascades tales of amber honeydew.

Fays are fled like last beams to hide in golden ages,
vanished crowns sink, lost in wavering rushes.

VILLAGE HALL COFFEE

Seeking a cup of coffee on
a hot spring day, more like June,
the thirteenth century pub is closed.
But the village hall door stands ajar.
Perhaps a jumble sale?
(Internal calculations,)
chances of coffee quite high.

And yes indeed, at least six women
sit round tables with flowery cloths.
No, not The Mother's Union,
or the W.I., or a committee, or
a women's only group.
It is a coffee morning! "Always Thursdays."
So I am welcome and biscuits too!

"Yes" the little shop will reopen
with volunteers and local produce.
Where do I come from?
My reply is met with dismay and sympathy,
and talked no more of.
Another knows where the bluebells grow
"Did you specially want to see the bluebells?"

The river and stepping stones are speculated upon;
are they dangerous, slippy, it looks deep and fast.
"You don't have dogs do you?
My friend had a dog ..." and she trails off to
enquire if I like the look of the concert advertised.
"Schubert, Handel, R.V.W."
Their village is honoured. "He's a well known name,
the pianist is excellent too!"

The other village down the hill, "has nothing,
no shop, no church, just a couple of sprawling farms really."
And yes, some of their plants did die, living so high
on the moor, all that ice and snow lying for weeks,
"A severe winter, it will have to be dug out!
The Japonica has double blossoms and the Wisteria,
ah the Wisteria!"

COUNTRY VERGE

Grass heads twitch,
  and a pale green hazel nut has
    fallen from the coppiced bushes.
It is so soft and warm in my hand.

But it's not as pretty as the baby
  rabbit I saw when we mutually
    startled one another:
brown eye to brown eye.

TRAVELLING AFTER FLOODS

Not so solid a black really, but
brown sloping worn topped trees
like besom brooms against
dusty sky.

Telegraph wires slice the scene
and barricades halve the road.
Vehicles make semi emergence
from spume cloud.

The windscreen wipers' soft
swishing forward, fall-back
a mesmerizing movement and
pattering rain.

Dun furrowed fields sodden.
Turret-trees, slit-eyeing their moats,
banks overflowing muckily brown
once again.

Gazing, a lessening light and
the land folds into itself, tucking shadows,
becomes more monochrome, above charcoal
mottled clouds.

SOUTH WEST TO PLYMOUTH

Pylons shackled scaffolds black,
back into the dusking distances,
their out reached arms weighted,
lines of Plymouth's energy.

Bright rubies strew the tarmac,
cigarette stubs from the lungs of Tartarus.

Protractor pulse protractor
degree smudged rotated cones.

Mist emergence the reticulated worm
sinews down the hill, flashing like a barber pole.

Parabola metronome of smears
torrent tempo, Spanish rain?

Emeralds square cut crème de menthe lagoons,
rills of black marble slipping away.
Starboard express, the night's platform
announces the next incomprehensible babble.

Pearls, necklace in abacus's cleavage.
Not yet grid locked,
good toes, naughty toes, down draft hot toes.

Intermittently crescent slowly
has halt.

Still stalking pylon giants
field striding in seven league boots.
Pompous about their job.

A solitaire,
westerly, calmly, illuminates the girders.

I SEE YOU WIND

I see you wind, now it snows,
  the snow dust dervish,
    swirling cyclones, like white
      semi-translucent spirits revealed
        skittering along the road.

I see you, Siberian wind sweeping
  powdered icy granules in sheets,
    driving them in waves;
      just like you raise an oar-shaped spume of froth
        across the restless breakers.

I see your misdemeanours –
  the fallen tree, (Ilex oak coffin blocks the track)
    unable to withstand the load of snow
      hurled by your forces.

You scour my face and make it sting.
You have outstayed your winter welcome.
Go! Visit some other friend!

WINTER HORSES

Motionless,
are they real?
All is frost-glitter.
Idyll of silver birch and mercury lake,
they seem still magic.
The Narnian ice witch has morphed
them to alabaster.
Then dawn's shell fingertips ripple their manes,
they breathe,
white life cloud ascending!

WITCHES

Winter chants, witches cackle,
put in their spells a clicking rattle
of bones and chattering teeth.

Add poisoned tongues with fungus
underneath and yellowing nails that scratch
and scratch and shriek.

Shred clouds to mares-tails
bend branches till they creak,
cast down all the leaves
in mouldy heaps.

In slimy clods
the leaves are earth-wards hurled,
and branches doubled till they snap
apart and splinter through the skies.

Detaching twiglets catch and scrape
scour nightmares' dappled tails and,
from an ever widening gash bleeds poisoned hail.

Grimly it precipitates arsenic-pale
craniums of shrunken grinning crones,
crunching, munching, salivating.

OLDEST WOODS

They looked unimpressive;
age is deceptive.
Gnarled and grey
bent by centuries of time
The Oldest Ones.
Trees of white coarse stubble
old man's whiskers,
frail as dandelion clocks
clinging brittlely onto life
in the crease of the hills
where the river trickles.

Ancient boulders with pale moss
grow from the ground, make dark secret holes
round your roots.
What have you copses seen?
What could you tell
if anyone still listened to the mutter
of your dry creaking voices?
Your sap has hardly risen,
soon you will be gone.

"Unless," the trees whisper persuasively
"something is done.
We are in no hurry,
we can wait,
we are not moved from our ways.
Stay with us, become a Dryad."

How exciting, deliciously tempting!
If I stayed
for you to renew and strengthen,
then would your branches be green again?
Would it be worth it?

Walk not with indifference
into the oaken spinney.
Clear the mind from voices!
Beware!
The Oldest Ones have hidden strength.
One knows not in innocence
the invocation of Pan who in this grove
still lingers with tenaciousness.

OUT OF BRACKEN

Chestnut horses breasted the forest's bracken,
and silver glinted the metal armour as birch trees.
They arose and advanced from the galloping
swiftness of morning mist when Apollo lifts the reins.

Iron shod hooves thudding, the snickering of bits,
stirrups, leather and black manes, rising and falling
and the splattering of mud droplets in arcs,
from the infrequent boggy greenways of Ashurst.

Then silence, except for an axe stroke afar
and two squirrels chasing about the treetops.

ROMAN DOG A.D. 168

On a shelf,
hand carved
a lopsided wooden dog.
And if it was ever painted
then it has worn off.

Pressed into
Daddy's palm,
as he sailed away with
the legions from Italy,
for Barbaric lands.

Hadrian's wall,
letters sent.
"How miserable and wet it was,
he missed their sunny loggia,
Bow-Wow woofs his love."

Life went on,
vines tended,
new tessellations laid.
Ordered into misty highlands
the dog sank in bog.

Bored at home,
learning parts
Marcus shielded his eyes as a
rider solemnly gave the news.
Then he howled, and howled.

AMBUSHED THOUGHTS

Trudging from the hill fort,
down the white bone clay track,
suddenly,
a charm of gold finches,
swift as fire blazed arrows,
flew straight across me
from a hawthorn thicket hide.

Perhaps I should have been
alert like the centurions,
their dusty studded sandals
marching in narrow columns.
Their eagle standard borne aloft,
flashing gold at every
twist of a tired wrist.

Would they have been
distracted by the pastel
shades of a rolling landscape?
Our woolly sheep that eat
plentiful green grass or
the sandy haired fox,
dug in waiting for
evening's cover.

Above the palisade, a full moon
is taut like the skin of a tabor.
Cohorts eat, laugh loosely and
booze beside their stinky
goat leather tents.
Close by Reynard prowls,
the owl silently kills,
the adder slithers,
bellying to the warmth
of their camp fires.

Then they were gone!
Their bird of prey rusting,
a serpent entwined about
its bronze remains.
And the Chalk-hill Blue
flitters on fragrant orchids in the sun,
and the lark arises higher
than Icarus and trills.

SEA-MASS

March tide gale, St Ives

It is out there;
The Sea.
I hear it heave,
its massive glassy weight,
tons of ice-green waters
that thrash buildings
built too close upon the shore.

For slatted eyrie
slate-roofed seagull nest
there's no immunity.
In prying wind-dark unconsciousness
of semi-sleep
it tumbles.
Sloshes humped forms tangled in white sheets.

Over the black cracked rock
breakers rush and retake.
Down below
pull currents under
wrap seaweed bladder-wrack that
binding, swaying, fringing
sombre caverns cling.

Seeping wind through-howls,
and thud of monotonous distance
vibrates un-giving granite forever,
rumbling depths fathom the ocean floor.
Dark hair fanned on pillow-bloated,
drowned in half sleep
of limbs, listlessly rocking lullaby
movement of water,
an eddying waltz.

Entwined with seaweed
barnacle slippers.
Flounce translucently jellyfish.
Night gale endures on and on
until exhausted stupor
lies upon the pale pink
chaise longue of dawn
untroubled.

PICK IT LILLY

Pick it Lilly, pick it Lilly, pick it Lilly
in the Spring my sweet in the Spring!

When the wind pulls hard at the sheets plying tying,
tugging, the wind in its youthful playtime.
Bone and spirit in the spars of moonshine
silver drenching, over reaching fingers between times,

unreal time of fading cross shadowed currents
when the Gibbous sails high like the tide
now in hazy zoned pink dawn light.

Oh pick it Lilly. Pick Lilly,
though unknowing what you're plucking
it's all forgotten, a misunderstanding
in the bustling, hard market harbour.

Silly non-urgent the empty shuttle jiggles in the race.
Pale shade to the wish bone fishes piled high, still
slippery in the sunlight.

Lilly Lilly Lilly

pick it in the Spring my love in the Spring!

Stitches and tacks needle in the waves
ever stitching and unpicking her life,
alone in the silver silken night.

And the youthful wind, so new in its prime time,
jaunty full of bounciness
kisses the sighs, cools the royal fingertips,
tugging at the winding sheet, ruffling her embroideries.

Pick it, pick it
it seams on endlessly,
so pick it in the Spring my sweet.

LADY SEA

Shot taffeta grey-green train,
smooth and silky yet crinkled,
light and dark laying on it,
lifting and rippling as it spreads.

The she of her edged with rock roses,
and a silver white stole higher up.
Deep beauty, passionately cold and irresistible,
a fitful challenge beyond all regulations.
A few more lost to her charms.

HARBOUR ENTRANCE

Steel sabre toothed canines they stand
and prong the scudding sky, brace
the harbour's mouth where
pewter sea gulps and gargles forth.

Stalagmitic masts that ricochet
wire-twanged sheets,
wind-spin the gyrating yachts' moorings
that yaw and pitch.

Abrasive the sea decays all hulls.
High tide, low tide, next spring tide,
hasten whilst shipshape
leave the quayside.

Slip away through ebb and flow.
Westerly winds whistle
wildly, shrilly, cast-off pipes.
Paean surf froths, liquidacious opus.

Cyan starved eyes from clammy pale skin;
finned, mithril, reptile tail agitates
the broiling waters: She lays-in-wait,
smiles, licks her lips…

ICY SEA

Icy sea, grey glacial
merging flows, cumulous chalk clouds
like mountainous bergs adrift.

Frost biting wind, skull compressing cold
Arctic waters in a Southern harbour
restless, deadly, misplaced,

like a captured polar bear.

BINOCULARS RAISED

Binoculars raised he stood with gleeful animation,
his dull spoil-sport spouse pulled her padded jacket closer.
I looked down the cliff
where a dark brown rock
made extending rings of water.
Odd happenings off Oddicombe beach …

"'Ere you, borrow these."
Into view sported the sleek seal,
nodding in and out the water's waves,
a young pup following!
Now I understand the excitement.

THREE TANKERS

Three orange tankers taking
shelter in the bay,
sea rough and grey
and white horses swirled their manes and stampeded.

Christmas Eve morning,
last night a Devon cliff-slide
crumbled to the tide.
White horses rolled their salty eyes and snorted.

Red mud-blooded water spreading
like a battle waged
between sea and land.
White stallions crashed about and cantered.

Three orange tankers anchoring
in the sheltered bay,
sea wild and grey.
Whistle and sing, riding white horses can't be delayed.

IN THE FIELD ABOVE THE SEA

They are gathered round the fire,
the temperature has dropped,
I seek a country pub and hot coffee.

They garner warmth from round the fire,
no coverings or rugs to wrap around.
I have my hat and gloves and woollen coat.

They huddle round the fire,
all day they'd roamed the field, eyes to the ground.
I've walked on greenways, enjoyed the ridges' heights.

Silently they stand around the smouldering fire.
Cinders shuffle, charcoal sparks pulsate,
I pass on by, yet stare with curiosity.

They are herding closer to the fire.
Flanks twitch; manes hang, at ease an angled hoof,
ashore the cold air rushes from the sea.

MIGRATION

Summer bronzed feet in sandals scythe
the long coarse grasses, dried brown straw
chaff which scrubs abrasively between toes.

Each thick bobbled tufted head gets stuck, wedged,
then bursts through, pings back flicking
calves which tread a swathe, an individual track
through parched knee-high stalks.

Burnished beige and blonde they bend to …
The Sun!

Drawn with forgotten ancient instincts,
Worshipers flock to the coastal cliffs
like migrating animals, seeking out moisture
when temperatures soar.

AN ENGLISH SUMMER

In England jumpers
go on and off every fifteen minutes.

This is August.
This is England.

I pack a jumper
just in case.

COOMBE CELLARS

By the estuary,
the water still recedes this afternoon,
and mud flats widen.
Ragged piles of seaweed scattered along it
and black headed gulls strutting,
with their doppelganger reflections.

Yellow floats bed into sand.
Shallows a crumpled taffeta confusion
of terracotta and sapphire;
as the low water tides out,
but sea determines to return.

It rises thirteen feet this night,
devouring the embankment,
black-hatted Isambard engineered.

WALKING TO ST SENARA'S

Taking the old path in late afternoon there's
heavy drizzle. The leaden pastel grey clouds
somnambulate over piled stone tors
and rolling hills of this changeful land.

Stone walls eroded by vigorous salt winds
fringed with dripping copper fronds,
frame a stile, four granite gateposts abreast,
a grating made with giant strength.

Several of these lead the feet of centuries,
the booted treads of time, or coffin bearers to
St Senara's, whose spires prop up mist and myth,
providing a merrymaiden's pew.

But also a plaque for John Davey from
Boswedneck to commemorate his possession
of "Considerable Traditional Knowledge of
the Cornish Language."

The grass glints bright with dark shadows behind
and dappled mossed boulders break the fields,
which slope to the rugged cliffs, and an
intense slit of white light, lines the sea's horizon.

MATTHEW'S SONG

from 'The Mermaid of Zennor'

Moon rise again, radiant moon you keep me guessing
so fickle, never in the same place or time each night.
When you fail to arrive all is dark and desolate,
the mournful sea sounds its dirge and is truculent.

Moon rise again, iridescent your skin gleaming
so fickle, this eve you show three quarters only quite.
When your silver shines and through the dark cloud percolates,
then my skin absorbs silver lustre that you lent.

Moon rise again, give pure visions and clear dreaming
so fickle, alter ingrained ways, show me what is right!
When harvest, months, and high sea tides follow your dictates
enchanter, I am your votive your gravitational migrant.

Moon rise again, your soft tender beams expressing
so fickle a love, waxing and waning in my sight.
When untouchable thronged with heavenly constellates
I am speechless; adore the silent loveliness you grant.

Moon rise again,
I am speechless adore the silent loveliness you grant.

MOON RISE AGAIN

We come and go
like stars twinkling,
meet and retreat
like sea on the strand.
Restless, unseen
love flies in the wind.

Moon rise again
another month gone.

Shadows of night
quietly kissing,
daylight that comes
with nobody there.
Coffees in cafes,
walks in the green woods.
Sit by the sea
listening to words.

Talking of things
politics, music,
deaths of our friends
new babies that come,
parents that age
grant forms and finance,
what exam marks?
Universities?

Driving around
timetabled journeys,
catch up at lunch,
perhaps a quick stroll.
Meetings readings,
try to write poems.

Full moon again
twenty eight days gone.

THE DAY RHODA DIED

Came thick wind-blown drizzle,
huge black branches scuffed the sky.

The crow heavy with rain flapped low
from hedge to hedge.

Across the tarn many white stiffened
waves, imitated the solitary swan.

From the train, marl tear-pitted sands
and jet necklaces of shiny slate-black rock.

Boats, stranded as the tide recedes
seemed frail, tottery on their keels.

The terminal text, the flying train higher
than gulls, waves breaking, breaking.

Dry stone walls edged square small fields
like, the neat knitted rows she made.

Curling mist reflected in smooth
lulled water, the opaque swan, whitest.

R.I.P. Rhodaleen Southcott
Friday 25th February 2011

AFTER CANCER

Knew he had been ill,
but I'd always thought of him secretly
as Gimli,
a doughty short tempered dwarf
with definite views.

(I know I shouldn't have, but you can't help your thoughts)
This was confirmed by his vociferous, avid
consumption of chilli cheese.

His house cut into the underside of a cliff,
containing rare rock slivers displayed
on the cavernous mantelpiece beside fossils.

With stubborn tenacity he laughs,
resumes his place amongst his
companions, questing energy.

But he seems too frail to
wield the weighty pickaxe.
Yet still he delves a lode
of poems.

MAYBE A SHAMAN?

A small kilted man
comes and goes
like moorland mist.
He drinks of the stream
and lives by the loch,
kens where he's needed
and knows who's been.

The highland cow
put its hoof through his drum
left on the heather roof of his home.

He sings of a babe swaddled in plaid
and simple things, fishes and bread.
Quotes childhood's dreams
not mercenary ways.

Gave fairy rock to hold fast fisted,
like you hold onto love
from the named depths of mountains
too odd to remember.
It doesn't matter: the point is symbolic,
of return to the Trossochs
some time again.

He saved the golden apple of ancient root
from the bulldozer when the guardians fled,
by orcharding it in trusted friends' gardens.
And yarns about Templars hidden in strongholds,
evading the might of a venomous pope.

He paced bare foot in a hostile city,
singing his truths in the ways of a bard,
percussion with stick and an empty milk carton,
when he hadn't a penny.

Full red wine in thistle cut glass was
a toast to enjoyment before leave taking, when
whispers wound down the spiral stone stairs:
"He's Shaman."

SCULPTOR'S STUDIO

Looking at sculptures
as two women poets
spoke about Moorland stone ...

smooth, muted pink
shiny, cold, adamantine.
A huggable shape
belies a weight too heavy to bear,
expel it!

Spasmed into a u shape
it can rock a grotesque lullaby,
and it will never be equal.
Placed on a plinth
one nose always looking down on the other,
clasped, co-joined, by a bloated belly
pro-formed in mould veining slipperiness.

And there is a hole this nihilism
funnelling to a smaller hole
on the other side.
Like rot decays gradual tedium under a molar.
Ugh it's like some slimy maggot!
Or some undeveloped thing
a foetus that has no chance at life.

It was conceived with a sensitive touch.
Wanted, prepared for
she listened to the rock,
went with it.
Formation following the contours.

CHANCE BONES

Those white bones,
and the rest under raging water.
One slipped hoof
was all it took,
and ribs rise fleshless like a wing.

On pale stones,
and the rest below rolling ocean.
One split sandal
flung back on shore,
and straps hang useless like bleached ribs.

Tall birch boles,
and the rest, sylvan rustling thicket.
One fallen tree
pulped to pages,
fans ribbed wings, soundless legends…

for the owl swoops silently
and spits out skulls.

SUNLIT LEAF

Pivot leaf,
caught on silver
cobweb thread.

Giddy for
today, so soon
you will fall,

like an oval copper shield
laid on comrades' leaf mould.

Sun now
strikes so splendid.

Bathe in it!

24, Forest Houses
Cookworthy Moor
Halwill
Beaworthy
Devon
EX21 5UU
www.indigodreams.co.uk